Questions and Answers: Countries

Colombia

A Question and Answer Book

by Kremena Spengler

Consultant:
Professor Maurice P. Grungardt
History Department
Loyola University
New Orleans, Louisiana

Capstone
press
Mankato, Minnesota

Fact Finders is published by Capstone Press,
151 Good Counsel Drive, P.O. Box 669, Mankato, Minnesota 56002.
www.capstonepress.com

Library of Congress Cataloging-in-Publication Data
Spengler, Kremena.
   Colombia : a question and answer book / by Kremena Spengler.
   p. cm.—(Fact finders. Questions and answers. Countries)
Summary: "Describes the geography, history, economy, and culture of Colombia in a
   question-and-answer format"–Provided by publisher.
   Includes bibliographical references and index.
   ISBN 0–7368–4351–5 (hardcover)
   1. Colombia—Juvenile literature. I. Title. II. Series.
F2258.5.S64 2006
986.1—dc22   2005001161

Editorial Credits

Silver Editions, editorial, design, and production; Kia Adams, set designer; Ortelius Design,
Inc., cartographer; Wanda Winch, photo researcher; Scott Thoms, photo editor

Photo Credits

Art Directors/A. Woodward, 12–13
Getty Images Inc./AFP/Rodrigo Arangua, 9
Kevin Schafer Photography, 1
One Mile Up, Inc., 29 (flag)
Photo Courtesy of Paul Baker, 29 (coin)
Photo Courtesy of Richard Sutherland, 29 (bill)
South American Pictures/Jason P. Howe, cover (foreground), 22–23; Mike Harding, cover
(background); Tony Morrison, 15
© The Nobel Foundation, 20
Victor Englebert, 4, 6–7, 11, 16–17, 18–19, 21, 25, 27

Artistic Effects:

Ingram Publishing, 18
Photodisc/PhotoLink/F. Schussler, 24

1 2 3 4 5 6 10 09 08 07 06 05

Table of Contents

Features

Where is Colombia?

Colombia is in northwestern South America. It is about three times larger than the U.S. state of Montana.

Colombia has many kinds of landforms. The Andes Mountains are in the west. Lowlands in the northeast are plains. The southeast is full of **swamps** and **rain forests**.

Rain causes floods along rivers in the rain forest.

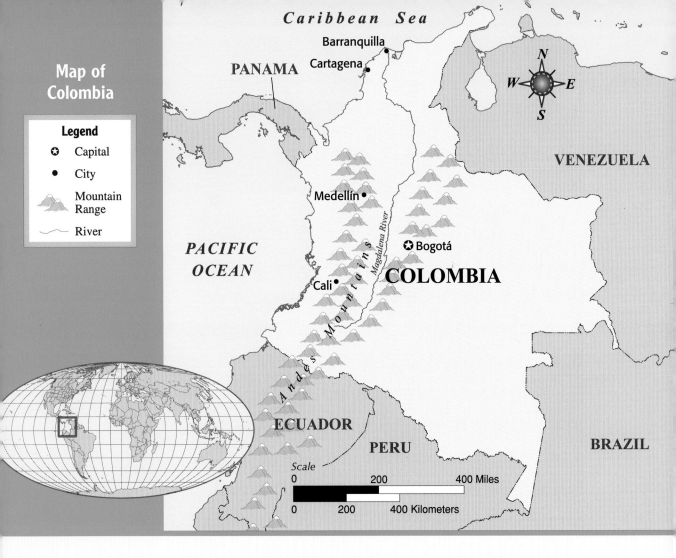

Map of Colombia

Legend
- ✪ Capital
- ● City
- ⛰ Mountain Range
- ∿ River

Caribbean Sea

Barranquilla

Cartagena

PANAMA

PACIFIC OCEAN

Medellín

Cali

Andes Mountains

Magdalena River

✪ Bogotá

COLOMBIA

VENEZUELA

ECUADOR

PERU

BRAZIL

Scale

0   200   400 Miles

0   200   400 Kilometers

N W E S

Colombia's climate stays the same throughout the year. Temperatures do not change much. It is always hot in the lowlands and cool in the mountains. Colombia receives a great deal of rain.

When did Colombia become a country?

Colombia became a country in 1810. It had been a Spanish **colony** since the 1500s. In 1810, people in the colony rose against Spanish rule. Simón Bolívar led Colombia's fight for independence.

Bolívar also led the fight for independence in other Spanish colonies. In 1819, Bolívar won against the Spanish in the Battle of Boyacá. Soon after, Bolívar united several former colonies into one country. It was called Gran Colombia, or Greater Colombia.

Fact!

Simón Bolívar is a hero in several South American countries. His army freed South Americans from Spanish rule.

This statue honors Simón Bolívar, the leader in Colombia's fight for independence.

Simón Bolívar died on December 17, 1830. By then, Gran Colombia had separated into three countries. They were Colombia, Venezuela, and Ecuador.

What type of government does Colombia have?

Colombia's government is a **republic**. Colombians vote for a president and vice president. They serve for four years. The president leads the country. If the president becomes sick, the vice president takes over the job.

A **cabinet** helps the president. The cabinet includes people from the two main political parties. They are the Liberal Party and the Conservative Party.

Fact!

Unlike many countries in South America, Colombia has held elections for most of its history.

Members of Colombia's National Congress sometimes meet with the country's president.

Colombia's National Congress makes the country's laws. It includes a Senate and a House of Representatives. Senators represent the whole country. Members of the House represent different regions. Congress meets twice a year in the capital, Bogotá.

What kind of housing does Colombia have?

Colombians live in many kinds of homes. Tall apartment buildings and large houses are common in cities and **suburbs**. Some homes are Spanish-style. They have red tile roofs. Some poor Colombians live in small homes. They do not have electricity or running water.

Where do people in Colombia live?

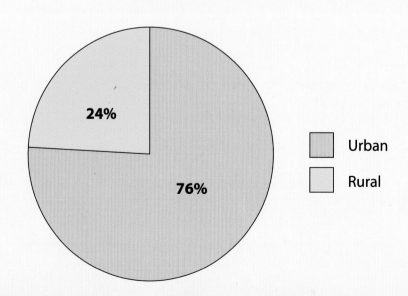

24%

76%

Urban

Rural

Spanish-style houses with red tile roofs line the streets of Villa de Leyva.

Colombian houses are different in each region. In warm and wet regions, families live in *tambos*. These houses have **stilts**. They are built high to let the breeze in and keep water and wildlife out. Homes in the Andes have thick clay walls to keep out the cold.

11

What are Colombia's forms of transportation?

Colombia has several highways and railroads. They connect cities in the mountains with cities in the lowlands. Many Colombians use buses to get from place to place.

High in the Andes, people use mules for transportation. Cable cars above the hilly land also move people and goods.

Colombia's location makes it easy to ship goods by water. Rivers such as the Magdalena are important transportation routes.

Fact!

Cities on the warm Caribbean coast have buses with open sides, to let in the breeze.

An Avianca plane prepares to take off in the city of Medellín.

It is hard to build roads through mountains and rain forests. Colombians must use planes for cross-country travel. The national airline is Avianca. It is one of the oldest airlines in the world.

What are Colombia's major industries?

Colombia's **natural resources** are used in its large mining industry. The land is rich in coal, copper, gold, and iron ore. Colombia mines the most emeralds in the world.

Colombian factories produce many goods. Cloth and clothing are two of the products made for **export.**

What does Colombia import and export?	
Imports	**Exports**
chemicals	bananas
grains	cloth and clothes
machines	coffee
mineral products	flowers
transportation equipment	petroleum

A worker in the flower industry cuts flowers inside a greenhouse.

Farming is a large industry in Colombia. Farmers grow bananas, corn, flowers, and sugarcane. Coffee is the country's main crop. It grows in a place called the "golden triangle," between the cities of Bogotá, Medellín, and Cali.

What is school like in Colombia?

Colombian children must go to school from ages 5 to 14. They take two years of kindergarten and five years of elementary school. After that, they may continue with two to six years of high school. Students who finish high school can enter a university.

Fact!

Children in warmer regions start and end school earlier in the day than children in cooler regions.

In the Choco Rain Forest, a Noanama Indian student teaches younger Noanama children.

Colombia has both public and private schools. Public schools are free. Some Colombian families pay for their children to go to a private school. Some poor children never finish school. They start work to earn money to help their families.

What are Colombia's favorite sports and games?

Soccer is the most popular sport in Colombia. Two popular teams are called Sante Fé and Millionarios. Most Colombians become fans of one of these teams at an early age. They remain fans for life.

The Colombian national team has played in several World Cup finals. They have also won the South American soccer championship seven times.

Fact!

On Sundays and holidays, the main street in Bogotá is closed to traffic so bicyclists can exercise. The best bikers ride up the Andes Mountains above the city.

Local farmers get together for a soccer game near the city of Cali.

Colombians enjoy the outdoors. They hike, climb, and ski in the Andes. On the coast, Colombians enjoy water sports. They fish, swim, water ski, and surf.

Bullfights are popular in Colombia. They take place year-round. Bullfights are dangerous for the matador who fights the bull.

What are the traditional art forms in Colombia?

Folk dances and music are enjoyed throughout Colombia. A lively type of music is salsa. It is played with maracas and horns.

Gabriel García Márquez is a famous Colombian writer. One of his books is about life in Colombia. It is called *One Hundred Years of Solitude*. This book is one of the most widely read books in Spanish.

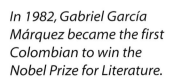

In 1982, Gabriel García Márquez became the first Colombian to win the Nobel Prize for Literature.

20

In 1979, painter Alejandro Obregon posed with some of his paintings.

Colombia has many respected artists. Alejandro Obregon painted animals and plants from the Caribbean region. Fernando Botero paints very large figures of other Colombians. His art and other painters' work are in Colombian museums.

What major holidays do Colombians celebrate?

Most Colombians are Roman Catholic. Christmas and Easter are very important. Colombians celebrate these holidays with processions and by going to church.

Colombians also celebrate national holidays. Independence Day is July 20. Cartagena's festival marks the city's independence from Spain. The festival has parades, dancers, fireworks, and a beauty contest.

What other holidays do people in Colombia celebrate?

Battle of Boyacá
Discovery of America
Epiphany
Labor Day
New Year's Day

Dancers enjoy performing during Carnival in Barranquilla.

Carnival celebrations take place in many Roman Catholic countries. Carnival is the last festive occasion before Lent.

Carnival in Barranquilla is one of the top five carnivals in the world. It lasts for four days before Lent. The city celebrates with parades, floats, and dance contests.

What are the traditional foods of Colombia?

Colombian foods are rich and seasoned. Many dishes have beef, chicken, or fish. They also use rice, potatoes, beans, and a root called yuca. Stews and soups are common meals. A famous soup is *ajiaco*. It is made with chicken, potatoes, corn, and avocado.

Fact!

Coffee is Colombia's national drink. Colombians drink coffee with most meals.

Colombians prepare a stew in corn paste, which will be boiled inside banana leaves.

Colombians like to cook with local food. Along the Caribbean Coast, people prepare meals with fish and coconut. In mountain valleys, people use potatoes grown there. People in western Colombia cook many meals with bananas.

What is family life like in Colombia?

Colombian families are close. Children and their parents may live in one home with grandparents, aunts, and uncles. Young people often live in the family home even after they marry.

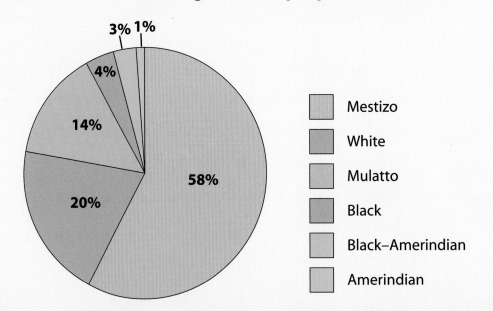

What are the ethnic backgrounds of people in Colombia?

- Mestizo
- White
- Mulatto
- Black
- Black–Amerindian
- Amerindian

3% 1%
4%
14%
20%
58%

A Colombian girl cuts her First Communion cake during a family celebration.

In Colombia, the father is often the head of the family. He earns a living, and the mother stays home to care for the house and children. In some families, both parents work outside the home. Others in the family group help at home.

Colombia Fast Facts

Official name:

Republic of Colombia

Population:

42,310,775 people

Land area:

*401,044 square miles
(1,038,700 square kilometers)*

Capital city:

Bogotá

**Average annual
precipitation (Bogotá):**

41.2 inches (104.6 centimeters)

Language:

Spanish

**Average January
temperature (Bogotá):**

*55 degrees Fahrenheit
(13 degrees Celsius)*

Natural resources:

*coal, copper, emeralds, gold,
iron ore, natural gas, nickel,
oil, silver*

**Average July
temperature (Bogotá):**

*55 degrees Fahrenheit
(13 degrees Celsius)*

Religions:

Roman Catholic	*90%*
Other	*10%*

Money and Flag

Money:

Colombian money is the peso. In 2005, one U.S. dollar equaled about 2,331 pesos. One Canadian dollar equaled about 1,938 pesos.

Flag:

The flag of Colombia has stripes of yellow, blue, and red. The yellow stands for Colombia's independence. The blue stands for the Atlantic and Pacific oceans. The red stands for the blood shed for independence from Spain.

Learn to Speak Spanish

Colombia's official language is Spanish. Learn to speak some Spanish words using the chart below.

English	Spanish	Pronunciation
good morning	buenos días	(BWAY-nohs DEE-ahs)
good-bye	adiós	(ah-dee-OHS)
please	por favor	(POR fah-VOR)
thank you	gracias	(GRAH-see-us)
yes	sí	(SEE)
no	no	(NOH)
How are you?	¿Cómo estás?	(KOH-moh ay-STAHS)
I'm fine	Bien.	(BEE-en)

Glossary

cabinet (KAB-in-it)—a group of advisers for the head of government

colony (KOL-uh-nee)—an area that is settled by people from another country and that is ruled by that country

export (EK-sport)—to send and sell goods to other countries

natural resource (NACH-ur-uhl REE-sorss)—a material found in nature that is useful to people

rain forest (RAYN FOR-ist)—a warm area where many trees and plants grow closely together because of heavy rainfall

republic (ree-PUHB-lik)—a government headed by a president with officials elected by the people

stilts (STILTSS)—posts that hold up a building above ground or water

suburb (SUHB-urb)—a town near the edge of a city

swamp (SWAHMP)—an area of wet ground

Internet Sites

FactHound offers a safe, fun way to find Internet sites related to this book. All of the sites on FactHound have been researched by our staff.

Here's how:
1 Visit *www.facthound.com*
2. Type in this special code **0736843515** for age-appropriate sites. Or enter a search word related to this book for a more general search.
3. Click on the **Fetch It** button.

FactHound will fetch the best sites for you!

Read More

Boraas, Tracey. *Colombia.* Countries and Cultures. Mankato, Minn.: Bridgestone Books, 2002.

De Capua, Sarah. *Colombia.* Discovering Cultures. Tarrytown, N.Y.: Benchmark Books, 2004.

Lopata, Peg. *Colombia.* Modern Nations of the World. Detroit: Lucent Books, 2005.

Owens, Caleb. *Colombia.* Faces and Places. Chanhassen, Minn.: Child's World, 2003.

Index